WHY LIBERALISM?

How our Sense of Empathy and Fairness Determines our Political Orientation

by Eric Balkan

Revision 2.5 7/18/11

Copyright 2011 by Eric Balkan
Published in the USA by Packet Press
ISBN 978-0-934741-10-1

Contents

Introduction

Think your political opinions are the result of carefully reasoned thought? Think that everyone would agree with you if they just weren't so clueless? Think again! Big government vs small government, free market vs a regulated market, individual freedom vs group benefits, conservative vs liberal.... Political controversies sound like they're based on differences in philosophy or ideology or maybe just fact. But they're not. The differences are largely cultural. And, in particular, they're based on how much a particular culture values empathy vs self-interest and fairness vs social stability.

This distinction between philosophy – commonly, how we choose to look at things -- and culture – the effect of all the varied influences on us during our lifetime -- is key. That's because philosophy is amenable to rational discussion, but cultural differences are not. They're part of us -- and much harder to change.

I got interested in this topic after some 40+ years of arguing politics without actually convincing anyone of anything. It finally occurred to me that our opinions on various political topics were based on deep-down, core beliefs, and not on the specifics of any particular issue. I then went off to study whatever thinking and research I could find on what those beliefs might be, and where they might have came from.

I became drawn to the conclusion that we obtain our beliefs largely from what behavioral/social scientists call the socialization process, via what cognitive science researchers call neural plasticity – which is what inculcates cultural influences into our brains. Further, I've theorized, the differences in our political beliefs stem from differences in how our various cultures and subcultures treat the attributes of fairness, empathy, self-interest, and social stability.

I should warn here that, while this book is inspired by current research, the interpretation of that research can vary. And this book is my interpretation: a theory if you will.

One of the side-effects of my conclusion was the realization that we can never be unbiased. So, even though I've made some attempt at it, in the interests of full disclosure, I admit to being a liberal.

I wrote this book both to better organize my own thinking on the subject by putting it into words, and to see what others thought of my theory. (My thanks to those, especially Howard Covin and my wife Freda, who have contributed feedback so far.) So, let's get started.

Social Stability vs. Fairness

Theory 1:

Conservatives seek to maintain the current social order, even if it's unfair.

Liberals seek to make things fairer, even if it upsets the current social order.

Virtually no one takes one of these positions to an extreme. We tend to each fall somewhere along the scale between wanting total stability and wanting total fairness. Take this situation: the police have arrested two people, one of whom is positively a terrorist and the other one an ordinary, innocent person. And it's impossible to tell which the terrorist is -- we just know that one of them is. If we release them both, the terrorist will continue his activities. If we imprison them both, we will be imprisoning an innocent man. If you say release them both, which is what our legal system would do, then change the situation so that there's 3 people, two of whom are terrorists. Do you still release them all? How about 6 people, where 5 are terrorists? 20 people? 100 people?

Or the other way, if you said lock them both up: If there are 10 people, and 1 is guilty, do you still lock them all up? You can play with these numbers until you find some you're comfortable with. And your numbers will undoubtedly be different than someone else's numbers.

A momentary detour: I use the terms social stability and social order largely interchangeably throughout this book. They're not quite the same thing, but they're parts of the same desire. And that is the desire, which we all have, to do things in the familiar way, in familiar settings. I suggest that this desire is simply greater in conservatives than in liberals.

And while we're at it, what is fairness exactly? The absence of bias is often given as a definition, but I don't think that goes far enough. For instance, if you were paid a salary not based on your work but on some random number chosen by a computer, that would not be biased, but it also wouldn't be fair. So fairness implies also a non-arbitrary relationship between actions and consequences. Taking both criteria together, it comes down to: getting what an unbiased observer thinks you deserve.

Now back to validating the theory. Think about Guantanamo. Conservatives want to continue keeping the inmates locked up, because it's safer that way. Liberals are concerned that some of those inmates are innocent, and we'll never know who they are if we don't have trials.

The above examples involved safety issues, but the same thinking gets involved in a very many political, social, and economic issues. Think about the issue of mortgage foreclosures. Where do you fall in siding with the banks that a contract is a contract, and siding with those who may have been taken advantage of by unscrupulous mortgage brokers, signing a contract that is perfectly legal but exploitative.

The issue of fairness comes into the mortgage situation because the average American – homeowner or prospective homeowner – does not have as much financial savvy as those who make a living selling financial instruments. This goes for stocks, bonds, mortgage derivatives, etc. Modern life is too complicated to ever know enough to match wits with the specialist on his own turf. This is likely to either bother you or make you shrug and say: caveat emptor – let the buyer beware.

The desire for social stability leads conservatives to reject all criticism of the current social order, whatever it is. This shows up in the popular slogan, used often during the Vietnam Era, but dating back at least as far as WWI: "If you don't like it here, leave".

Some would like to decide these kinds of questions by absolute rules that involve the use of words like "always" and "never". But that is not terribly useful, often depends on an unshakeable faith in principle of some sort, and is the kind of rigid fanatic thinking that seems robotic and inhuman -- because it is. Except for those joining cults, most of us are not built to accept anything unconditionally. Real life is never black and white, all or nothing. In fact, human beings are not terribly rational, which we'll get into more in a bit. We'll also see a lot more examples of social stability vs fairness, after we look at the other major building block of our political orientation.

Self-Interest vs Empathy

Theory 2:

Conservatives seek to enhance their situation, even at the expense of others.
Liberals seek to enhance everyone's situation, even at their own expense.

We laugh when others laugh, feel sad when others cry.... There actually is a neuroscience basis for "I feel your pain". We have an "empathy circuit" in our brain. (Simon Baron-Cohen, The Science of Evil). This involves a number of different structures in the brain, working together. Among these are "mirror neurons" that fire when we see someone doing something, like a physical activity or expressing an emotion. Whether it's a pro hitting a tennis ball or the fear of a child (and his parents) who's fallen down a well, our brains are reproducing some part of that experience inside our heads.

Think about a movie you've seen or a story you've read. Was there a character to whom you related, who faced obstacles that you were rooting for him or her to overcome? Even if that character was nothing like you, there was something about that character that triggered an empathetic response in you. Maybe he/she was the underdog, or a victim of unfairness, or possessed some admirable trait.

This empathy is also in play when we're members of a group. Humans are joiners. We want to be a member of something larger than ourselves: a family, a group of friends, a group at work, a religious group, a nationality. Being a member means distinguishing between members and not-members. (The human race is not seen as a group, because nobody is excluded.) The nature of a group means that the members have some bond that outsiders don't. This is the basis of our Us vs Them attitude. Even where there is no physical or cultural distinction between ourselves and others, we will create one. E.g., fans of sports teams, Facebook friends....)

As a member of a group, we can get more accomplished than as an individual by ourself. An obvious example is a marriage, where responsibilities are often divided. In rural settings, children also have work roles assigned to them. Businesses and other organizations depend on employees/members to work together as a group. A nation, when attacked from outside, can pull together as a group -- if the citizens feel some bond among themselves that excludes the enemy.

The downside is that this easily can carry too far: ethnic grouping turns into racism, feelings of nationalism turn into imperialism. (Imperialism being the feeling that how your nation does things is best, and everyone else should follow your example.) Not only is imperialism unfair, but it's counter-productive in the long run because "The Others" start developing a counter-nationalism that's antagonistic to yours. (Hobson, Imperialism, 1902)

But how does empathy relate to political viewpoints? Different cultures vary in the amount of empathy they instill in their members. (There are also individual differences within a culture, but I'm going to show that the big differences that are meaningful in politics are cultural differences.)

Conservative cultures have less empathy than liberal cultures. Their "Us" is a smaller group. They're prone to form less diverse groups than liberals, because their empathy does not extend far to people who look, talk, and think differently. Liberal cultures are more apt to be cosmopolitan and inclusive. At least part of this is just geography. The hunter or farmer is less dependent on others than the urban dweller. The farmer is largely a self-sufficient generalist, the urban dweller usually has a specialized vocation and is interdependent with others who are specialists, many of whom may be members of diverse groups. The urban dweller, for instance, cannot get food, fuel, transportation, etc., without depending on the activities of others. Interestingly, the urban family, more dependent on market activities than the rural family, is often less enthusiastic about the benefits of an unregulated/free market than is the rural family.

The opposite of empathy can be thought of as self-interest. (As much as any emotion can have an opposite.) Effectively, "Us" becomes "Me". Taken to this extreme, it can become sociopathic, as with serial killers and career criminals. At this level, there is, to borrow from Prof Baron-Cohen, no affective empathy at all, no ability to put yourself into the other guy's shoes. Fortunately, this is unusual. No culture can exist for long without some amount of empathy, often expressed in economic relationships that go beyond the dollars involved. But different cultures promote different amounts of empathy.

To be fair ☺ I have to mention that research by Prof Baron-Cohen indicates that autistic children seem to have neither cognitive empathy (ability to read others' emotions) nor affective empathy (ability to feel other's emotions). Their empathy circuit is out-of-whack, to use a scientific term. ☺ In this case, this physical inability to relate to others produces a kind of detached self-involvement.

But this is different from a career criminal, such as a con artist, who can in fact read others' emotions, and use those emotions against his victim. Perhaps he can do this because he is not capable of feeling those emotions—zero affective empathy -- or perhaps because he has repressed or rationalized away those emotions, having unconsciously learned to do this via cultural influences. (I'll get into socialization via neuro-plasticity later on.)

In feudal times, the lord was considered to have a responsibility to his serfs and peasants – noblesse oblige. When industrialization came about, the new lords were businessmen who hired workers the same way they bought machinery, with no obligation to either. One such businessman, David Ricardo, was instrumental in introducing ideas that justified this lack of empathy, becoming the foundation of the new capitalism. E.g., that profits and wages are inversely related. (Market economies have existed since the dawn of time, but it was 19th century economists who created economic laws which assumed markets were rational, and could thus be analyzed with differential equations, and further that these laws were no more influenced by human emotion or governmental action than the laws of physics.)

Even though we've gotten far from the capitalistic concept of how business should treat workers -- there's no more child labor, we have weekends off, there are safety regulations in workplaces -- there is still a conservative-libertarian culture that holds this lack of empathy, and this concentration on self-interest, as the ideal way of conducting business. (E.g., in the novels of Ayn Rand.) More on this later.

Of course, for nearly all of us, this is not an either-or proposition. Poor people will vote for bigger benefits and rich people will vote for tax cuts. Oil rig workers will probably vote for less regulation of oil drilling platforms, if they think it will cost jobs, while tourists will probably vote for more safety regulation, if they think a spill will spoil their vacation.

A current political hot-potato that falls outside my theory is the coal mining situation in West Virginia, where the self-interest of those losing their traditional hunting/fishing grounds and whose children are getting sick from coal dust, are opposed by coal miners afraid of losing their jobs if the mining was further regulated. (A conservative approach would let the market work it out between these two interest groups, decided on their respective economic power. A liberal approach would be to seek out a fair resolution.)

I also have to admit I believe in the saying that "a program for the poor is a poor program" because the constituency to support it will never be very large. (Self-interest trumping empathy.) That's why, of all the programs for the poor introduced by FDR's "New

Deal" in the 1930s, the few that survived, like social security, benefit everyone, and not just the poor.

Nonetheless, we all sacrifice our self-interest to some extent -- serving in the military, paying taxes, etc -- if we're asked to do it in a fair way. That is, while few would oppose paying a tax to support a public school -- at least in this century -- we would object if some significant number of people got out of paying it. Ditto for military service. Back in the 1860s, when Abraham Lincoln instituted a draft to fight the Civil War, it was possible for the sons of rich people to pay their way out of it, a factor in the anti-draft riots that erupted at the time. (Also the rationale for instituting a draft lottery during the Vietnam War, instead of automatically deferring college students.)

So, then, self-interest can be ameliorated by both considerations of empathy and by considerations of fairness. This muddles a bit the clean division I made between the fairness-social stability axis and the empathy-self-interest axis, but that's to be expected in the real world where nearly everything eventually interacts with everything else.

A personal sidebar here: I began studying empathy after I got interested in how, throughout history up through the present day, massacres and even all-out genocides could take place. I decided to analyze this through the process of writing a novel. I picked medieval Central Asia because the Turco-Mongol nomads of Genghis Khan and others like him were responsible for a number of very large, very brutal massacres. (And, to be honest, the military aspects were fascinating.)

I could understand why a political leader might exterminate the population of a city – as an example for others – but why did the individual soldiers sign up for it and willingly participate? My study of the period, and the working out of the characters' motivations in City of Tears, showed that there could be many factors: loyalty, obedience, peer pressure, glory, adventure, greed, revenge…. But there was one underlying factor: the Us vs Them dynamic. I.e., an almost complete lack of empathy for the victims.

The victims just weren't viewed as people to be concerned about. There's an old nomad expression that goes something like: Myself against my brothers, my brothers and I against the clan, the clan against the tribe, the tribe against the world. I suspect that a competition for scarce resources – the nomads constantly fought among themselves for the best pastureland – leads to a culture with lower empathy than a culture where there's enough to go around. (Though this doesn't explain the Romans. Oh, well.)

We can see from these examples that self-interest has been an important factor in political issues, but it comes at the expense of ignoring empathy for others.

At this point you're probably thinking one of the following:

> 1 - This is great stuff
>
> 2 - The author is just restating the obvious
>
> 3 - Some of this might be true

4 - It's complete hogwash

All of these reactions can be -- wait for it -- counter-productive. (They may also say more about you the reader than me as the writer.) Ideally, a paper or book of ideas should be approached the same way that jurors are instructed in a trial: to reserve judgment. The reason being that if you make a judgment early on, it will color what you get out of the rest of the work. You'll start reading into the work what you expect to see in it. A better approach is to try and keep your mind clear and unencumbered while seeking to understand what the author is saying, and then at the end, when you've understood what he's saying and why he's saying it, you're then qualified to both pass judgment on it and take from it anything that could be useful. That's my take on it, anyway.

I will give you a hint of what this is all about, though. That liberalism is about making decisions based primarily on fairness and empathy. And that a society structured along those lines will benefit more people, and to a higher degree, than a society structured along any other lines.

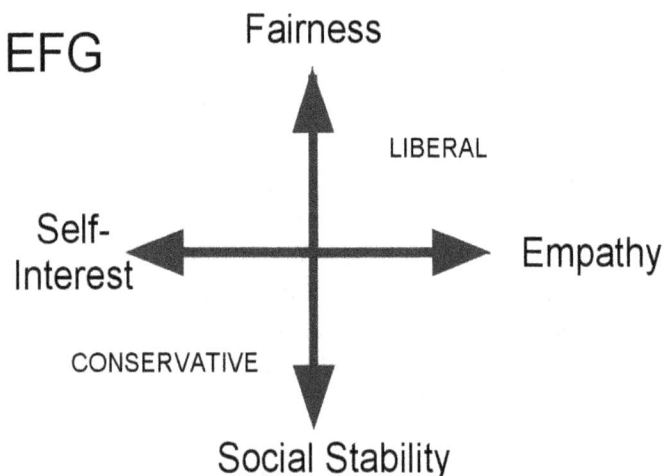

EFG

Picture fairness vs social stability as one axis and empathy vs self-interest as another axis on an x-y graph, as shown above. The result is what I call an Empathy-Fairness Graph, or EFG for short.

Alternatively, you can think of this as a compass – your political compass, if you will. Fairness is due north, social stability is its polar opposite, so to speak. Ditto for empathy vs self-interest. Liberalism resides in the NE, conservatism resides in the SW. (The relationship to the map of the US is purely coincidental.) Among conservatives, religious conservatives would fall to the South, while financial conservatives more to the West.

Placing an individual or a group as a dot or a cloud somewhere on the graph/compass can be helpful in many cases, but probably should not be used in isolation. Individuals are too complex and groups too amorphous -- shifting too much – for any tool to work 100% of the time. I offer the EFG as a way to better understand the different sides of a political dispute. Take the current dispute over Medicare. The current Medicare plans are being attacked on pragmatic grounds of financial instability, but in fact, those who oppose Medicare would oppose it no matter how financially stable it is. E.g., I would not be surprised to find out that the politicians who complain about Medicare fraud are the same ones who refuse to allocate money for fraud investigators.

To give you an idea of how I arrived at these two opposite pairs of cultural-based political positioning, consider the Soviet Union before it collapsed. Hardline communists who wanted to maintain the Soviet Union were referred to as conservatives, while their opponents attempted to "liberalize" the system. These labels were not semantic accidents. They represent the desire to hold on to what you've got and to continue "traditional" ways of doing things, vs realizing that the system is not treating the bulk of the public well or fairly. EFG.

To take an example from American history: during the Civil War, Southern men enlisted and fought for a system that promoted slavery even though most did not own slaves. They were defending the way things were. Their fear was that freeing the slaves, making blacks equal to whites, would be the end of the South as they knew it. At the same time, they thought of themselves as rebels, because they were fighting authority – a "foreign" authority they saw as wanting to change the social order.

Human beings love pecking orders. We often want to rank ourselves against others. By establishing blacks as a permanent underclass, poor white Southerners could feel better about themselves, even if they were at the very bottom of white society. We can see this attitude after the war, when Southerners conceded a military loss but were unable to change their culture. They created segregation, enforced often by Jim Crow laws but mostly by attitude. (Washington DC had no Jim Crow laws but carried on, e.g. school segregation, as if there were.)

This culture persisted into the 1960s, where an individual's position on racial integration was largely determined by culture, which in turn was determined by geography. Despite all the attempts at rational argument during this period, the issue was essentially fought over cultural grounds -- and specifically the cultural attributes I've mentioned -- much as the Civil War had been fought 100 years earlier.

To give a further example of culture determining politics, there's President Woodrow Wilson. Considered a progressive who fought for issues like women's right to vote, he was also, being a Southerner, an ardent racist who segregated the federal civil service: reportedly so that white women wouldn't have to work with black women.

Another impetus for my investigations was realizing that the traditional Left-Right distinction is often not useful. For instance, often in the last century, fascism and monarchism were referred to as right-wing and communism as left-wing. The Russian Revolution, for instance, was viewed as a move from an extreme right-wing political system to an extreme left-wing political system. Yet, for the average man in the street, the differences were largely superficial. When he went to work every day, he reported to a boss he didn't vote for, followed organization policies and procedures he had no say in, got paid whatever the bosses said they'd pay him, worked the hours they said he should work, fought in the wars the government said he should....

To be honest, I do have to say that Czarist Russia was so repressive -- treating it subjects as sub-human -- that anything was an improvement. And there was certainly an improvement in the social safety net under communism than under czarism – even Hitler's Germany had a social safety net -- but when you come right down to it, on any measure of personal freedom, there wasn't much difference between the Czar and Stalin. Or between Hitler and Stalin. We can say that all these systems had low EFG values.

Left and Right, Liberal and Conservative, are labels. Labels are handy mental shortcuts. We see the word, and we immediately form a mental picture of it, and then don't think about it further. That's often useful. And often not. Because often this stereotyping keeps us from actually thinking about what an issue is about. Assign the word liberal to an issue, and conservatives will automatically condemn it, whatever its merits. And vice versa for liberals.

A classic instance of this occurred shortly after Bill Clinton had taken office as president in 1992. Clinton introduced a health care plan that he and wife Hillary had worked out. But it was dead-on-arrival, and DOA exactly because their name was on it. Now, here's the interesting part. A reporter for the pre-Murdoch Wall Street Journal took the Clinton health care plan, removed the Clintons name from it, and asked people what they thought of it. A typical response: "Now this is a good plan, not like the Clintons' plan."

But I don't expect people to stop using labels. What I'd like to do is: Discard the use of left-right, as often meaningless. AND Redefine liberal and conservative according to my fairness-social stability and empathy-self-interest axes, i.e., EFG values.

Of course, as I will freely admit, people are inconsistent, may misunderstand an issue, and often won't fall neatly into a place on the EFS. But it's still more useful than current analyses where neither side understands the other.

I've offered EFG not as an explanation of Everything, but as a guide in understanding political causes. While many political arguments get involved with policy specifics -- e.g., how many dollars does a program cost, what are the protections against fraud, etc. -- the real issue is the cultural divide. Pick an issue and look at it with this paradigm: that people take sides in a political question based on fairness vs social stability, empathy vs self-interest.

Now, while I said earlier that conservatives try to maintain the current social order, I have to expand that. (Because simple answers when human behavior is concerned are often too simple.) It's not necessarily the current social order that people will defend, but their mental picture of it. That's often not the same thing. Because all of us see what we expect to see, i.e., what culture has engrained us to see. So we can find ourselves standing up for something that never actually existed, like the idealized world of Ronald Reagan's childhood or a 1950s sitcom. Or maybe it's memories from when we were younger – the "good old days" that always seem better than they were – not necessarily because they were, but often because we were more optimistic and resilient when we were younger and failed to see or understand all the problems.

Common Alternative Explanations

Individual Responsibility

Let's continue now with some seeming exceptions to my EFG picture. First, there's the conservative stress on individual responsibility; that people should be accountable for their actions. This certainly seems reasonable. And so it is. It's actually something we all feel, though we express it in different ways. What's peculiar to conservatives is that they've seemingly defined individual responsibility as the responsibility of other people. Because conservatives score low on fairness questions, they are apt to criticize others for behavior they engage in themselves.

Let's look into this more closely. Conservatives typically complain about government handouts, that people shouldn't depend on government for daily life. Yet, a Washington Post study after the 2000 election showed that every state which voted for George W Bush, the red states, received more money from the federal government per capita than it paid in taxes, while every state that voted for Al Gore, the blue states, paid more in taxes than it got in benefits. (Don't think that telling this fact to conservatives will affect their thinking, because it's culture that counts, not facts. They will immediately try to dispute it, rather than thinking about it or researching it for themselves.)

So, while conservatives oppose, say, aid to cities, they have no problem with corn price supports, subsidized hydroelectricity, and the plethora of useless military bases which the Pentagon would like to close, but can't, because they bring federal money into some congressman's district. Self-interest.

It's not just politically that conservatives demonstrate individual irresponsibility. Think about who it is who drives drunk, who leaves trash in parks, who is unconcerned about the effects of second-hand tobacco smoke or global climate change... it's the people who are low on empathy and fairness scales, and high on maintaining the current way of doing things, no matter the consequences.

Here's a little historical tidbit, not taught in schools. During the 1930s Great Depression, when many American investors felt it too risky to invest in the U.S., they invested money in the one country that was doing well during the global depression: Nazi Germany. In a triumph of self-interest over individual responsibility, and in particular the dictum that actions have consequences, money from individual American investors as well as 16 major US companies like Ford and IBM, helped Adolf HItler build an industrial base that would eventually be turned against the US and be used to kill American soldiers.

Worse, perhaps, is the complete lack of any acceptance of responsibility for this mistake. Not a single mea culpa or even "my bad".

Nor do conservatives learn from this. During the Cold War, we supported dictators and fanatic religious groups around the world if they opposed

Soviet communism. Among former allies we armed whom we later ended up fighting, there's Saddam Hussein and the Taliban. But there was also something else working here. Despite America having been born in revolution, we became the enemy of revolution. As conservatives came to dominate foreign policy, the goal shifted to maintaining the current social order, the perceived American way of life, or the conservative mental picture of the American way of life (which did not include blacks, gays, "feminists" and so on). No matter how unfairly people were being treated overseas, we supported the status quo.

In Southeast Asia, the Vietnamese fought for self-determination and independence against the French, the Japanese invaders, the French again, US backed dictators, and finally the US itself. No empathy on our part. No sense of fairness. Even liberal presidents found themselves largely helpless when attempting to confront what President Eisenhower called the "military-industrial complex". (Eisenhower had warned against getting involved in a land war in Asia, but not being considered a true conservative, his advice -- now 3 such wars later -- was largely ignored.)

I haven't read George W Bush's new book, but I'll bet he found it very hard, if not impossible, to accept the blame for any of the many mistakes of his administration. Not accepting responsibility for a mistake you've made is irresponsible, by definition. So a conservative desire to see individual responsibility is in fact a desire to see others be held responsible, and not themselves. This can be

understood in terms of a lack of empathy and a lack
of fairness. It's also counter-productive, because you
don't learn anything if you don't recognize your
mistakes. After all, everyone makes mistakes -- I'm
probably making some mistakes in this book -- so
what's critical is what you do after you realize you've
made one: deny it, ignore it, or fix it and keep from
making the same mistake again.

Political Correctness

This is an odd one. Conservatives say that there
is too much concern over hurting people's feelings --
too much empathy -- that people should be able to say
what they want, even if it's not in good taste. But
these are often the same people who will look to hit
you with a 2x4 if you make "incorrect" remarks about
God or George Bush. When Michael Moore did an
expose of George W Bush in Fahrenheit 911, he was
labeled anti-American by conservatives. But
conservatives don't consider this shushing of criticism
to be political correctness. They are simply anti-
empathy, not pro-free-speech.

This provides us an additional insight into
political thinking: conservatives tend to be less self-
aware than liberals. That is, they believe things and
do things, without thinking about why they believe
them and why they do them. This makes sense if you
go back to the desire for social stability. Having a
stable society means that you will pick up the
attitudes of those around you without having to think

about them, because they've worked in the past. (Or seem to have.)

Something for Nothing

It often seems that conservatives will get upset at the mention of someone, somewhere, getting something for nothing. Well, it's certainly unfair for someone to get something for nothing. But why do conservatives seem to get more upset over this than liberals? Aesop may have put his finger on it some 2000 years ago in the fable of the ant and the grasshopper. The ant worked hard all summer building his anthill and putting food away for the winter, while it was party, party, party for the grasshopper. Then when winter came, the party was over, and the grasshopper was left out in the cold.

Conservatives feel the grasshopper shouldn't ask for help from the ant, not so much on the grounds of fairness, but because the grasshopper's lifestyle was a living rejection of the ant's social order: an order based on reward for work done. No work, no reward. The liberal will feel some empathy for the grasshopper, hoping that the grasshopper will learn his lesson and make better decisions next time -- anyone can make a mistake, after all. But the conservative, with a lower empathy scale, will not be as charitable. (Interestingly, conservatives feel that government should not support the poor, but that the poor should instead rely on private charities. I guess they expect the contributions to those private charities to come from empathetic liberals.)

Respect for Authority

Conservatives often say that they are more respectful of authority and a hierarchical system that supports authority, than liberals are. And are often accused, by liberals, of being too respectful to authority. Some research exists which seems to back this up. But how true is it?

During the Vietnam War, conservatives got upset with the harsh liberal/radical verbal attacks on the President. (First LBJ, then Nixon.) Their feeling, they said, was that the President deserved respect simply by being president. Consequently, they had difficulty believing "Tricky Dick", as Nixon was once dubbed, was actually as tricky as his critics claimed. Ditto for the Bush administration being as impossibly inept as it proved to be.

Yet conservatives mercilessly attacked Bill Clinton from the beginning of his presidency, especially when he indicated he would change the policy towards gays in the military. And attacks on President Obama for being a non-nativeborn Muslim radical liberal racist gangster demon socialist were unrelenting – at least until he started sounding like a conservative. Even the First Lady has taken flack for saying that schoolchildren eat too many sweets.

In fact, there's an anti-authoritarian streak among conservatives raised to believe that America is the land of the free. Think about the movie "Smokey and the Bandit", or anyone who thumbs his nose at "the system". Like the Southern rebels of the Civil War, these people are rebelling against an authoritarian system imposed from above, but they're not rebelling against the day-to-day system they've grown up in. (Which is why the moonshiner and the sheriff were on the same side during the '60s civil rights protests.) Like the teen drug dealer to a cop in the TV series, "The Wire": we sell drugs and you bust us, that's how it works. Don't go messing that up. (Not an exact quote, but you get the picture.) So when The Bandit outfoxes Smokey, or when the Dukes put one over on Boss Hogg, that's actually a revalidation of the conservative image of The American Way, so to speak.

That hierarchies are not related to political thinking can be seen in academia. While it's generally accepted that faculty members in the liberal arts are overwhelmingly liberal, they're part of a hierarchical system of status and titles. E.g., you can be a great teacher, but if you're not a professor, you don't have the status of someone who is. Conversely, on Wall Street, a bastion of conservatism, how much money you can make for your company is more important than your title.

So what's going on here? I would say that a respect for authority and hierarchy is not a fundamental decider in political decisions. It depends almost entirely on whether the authorities in question support the existing social structure or are viewed as opposing it. Or, maybe putting it another way, conservatives have respect for the authority of the social order, including religious doctrine and the military chain of command, but not for the individual holding that authority if he departs from traditional practice.

Faith-based Politics

There are any number of "litmus test" issues that separate conservatives and liberals. One is the reaction to the concept of global warming, or more inclusively, global climate change. I find three basic objections to the concept, all based on faith of some sort:

1 - Religious faith. It's just not possible, change-deniers say, that God was so short-sighted as to create a world that can become inhospitable to man. God either wouldn't allow that, or will supply a brand-new world when the time is right. Or maybe Jesus will take us all up to Heaven before it happens. (Well, he'll take Christian conservatives up, anyway.)

2 - Faith in the Free Market. "The free market can solve all problems, but the free market has no way to respond to global climate change, so global climate change must not be a problem." I'm not being facetious here, unfortunately. A concomitant argument is that we would have to sidestep the "free" market to do anything about global climate change, and we don't want to do that, so let's not do anything about global climate change.

3 - Faith in technology. Some people, on various parts of the political spectrum, have the same uncritical attitude towards technology that Homer Simpson has towards donuts. It can do aaanything. Well, good luck with that.

There is another attack on the global warming concept, which is more subtle. Like Creationists who have learned they can't win by attacking science directly and so have opted to confuse the issue by referring to Creation as science, this approach says that there is no proof that global warming is man-made, and if it's natural, we shouldn't do anything about it. (Fortunately, no one adopts this kind of pseudo-reasoning when they see a hurricane or tornado coming.)

But how do political questions like this end up being decided by faith? Because faith in the current system -- religious, political, economic -- is one of the two foundations of conservatism. It's culturally engrained in the nature of conservatives. It's what keeps conservatives supporting a social order no matter what defects in it are pointed out. In fact, critics and whistle-blowers are denigrated for daring to even raise the question. So the good conservative will not only disbelieve a game-changer like global warming, but will feel real anger towards anyone even suggesting it. "If you don't like it here..."

Big Government vs Small Government

But what about the recent election in 2010, with its constant media barrage of articles, news reports, surveys and campaign ads about big government vs small government. That sounds like a philosophical issue. But, again, looking beneath the surface, we can see something else. First, by way of background:

The original distinction between what later came to be called Right and Left often centered on government. The Right favored the traditional means of government: hereditary monarch supported by an aristocratic elite. The Left emerged as a counter force, seeking change. This counter force originally included businessmen who wanted government out of economic affairs -- "Classical Liberalism" -- but businessmen would eventually switch sides, as those among them who became wealthy became the new power elite. As business turned to government for help in ensuring their status -- e.g., making labor unions illegal -- the Left became more representative of the working class.

This anti-government attitude was expressed by, for instance, Karl Marx, who viewed government as the tool of the ruling class. After capitalism had produced enough goods for everyone, a socialist system could be introduced in which everyone would be in the same class. With no ruling class, the state would then "wither away". To be clear, Marxism is not anarchism, which is why anarchist icon Emma Goldman was not a Marxist, and even Marx himself said he wasn't a Marxist.

Lenin and Stalin, unfortunately, would later turn this disdain for the state on its head, making government all-powerful. In his last book, Leon Trotsky wrote that the Soviet Union had swapped one elite for another, the new one being the Communist Party bureaucracy. (Though it would have been much better if he'd realized this earlier.)

It was this kind of government, and that of the fascist systems arising elsewhere in Europe in the 1920s and '30s, that inspired the rise of anti-state libertarians like Ludwig von Mises and Ayn Rand, who viewed government as the enemy of freedom, much as Marx had decades earlier.

During the 19th century, the US was torn between contrary attitudes towards government: defending the elite vs defending those who could not defend themselves. When Abraham Lincoln freed the slaves, and General Sherman gave them land appropriated from the plantation owners, it was an extension of government power on a larger scale than anything seen before in the U.S. After all, the original framers of the Constitution had put a high regard on property rights and contract law. I.e., if you paid for something, including a slave, it was yours, and the government couldn't take it away.

With Lincoln's assassination, though, the government went back to protecting property rights over human rights. President Andrew Johnson restored land rights to what they had been before the Civil War. While the slaves had been freed by Lincoln, and slavery was now illegal, the freed slaves got not only no land, but no farming tools, no farm animals, no seed, no money or credit to buy seed --

and no way to support themselves other than working as sharecroppers (tenant farmers) on the same plantations where they had been slaves. (Nightriders and local authorities, with the tacit approval of President Johnson, terrorized the freed slaves into staying on the plantations.) Many Congressional Republicans took exception to this, but over the next hundred years, government in the South meant maintaining the status quo.

Also, in the 19th century, government in the US more and more defended the right of business to operate as it liked. Even though the Constitution gave no rights to corporations, conservative judges actively created case law benefiting business. At its worst point, labor strikes were considered illegal as being "in restraint of trade". Unions were often considered illegal as interfering with the contract between an employer and an individual worker. Both in the US and Europe, pro-business government was opposed by social reformers, the new progressives, and by revolutionaries.

This situation continued in the U.S. until reformers, like Theodore Roosevelt, managed to wrest control of the government away from business interests. Arguing that everyone deserved a "square deal", government became the ally of the ordinary citizen instead of his enemy. But not for long, as President Taft and later the Republican Party of the Roaring Twenties turned about to favoring business again. But that policy and the resulting rising income inequality eventually caused a bubble economy that was suddenly punctured. In the 1930s, Franklin Roosevelt, considered by the rich as "a traitor to his class", again turned government from being a defender of the elite to being a defender of the general public. "Governments can err; Presidents do make mistakes,... but better the occasional faults of a Government that lives in a spirit of charity than the consistent omissions of a Government frozen in the ice of its own indifference."

The Roosevelt legacy -- both of them -- has persisted into modern times, where progressives turn to government to ensure fairness, while conservatives turn to government to ensure social stability, e.g. anti-terrorism security and internment policies, support of repressive foreign dictators, outright military intervention overseas, laws against recreational drug use, and even laws against online poker playing -- but against government where it's viewed as upsetting the domestic social order.

Please forgive this oversimplification of American history -- hard to cover a couple of centuries in a few paragraphs -- but I think you can see that there is no real philosophical issue here of large vs small. During WWII, the federal government became hugely powerful without much objection by most conservatives, because it was generally agreed it needed to do so.

Size doesn't matter. :-) It's what the government does that's critical: in considering policy, where on the EFG is it? And that is determined by which cultural group is in charge.

Sense of Duty

James Q Wilson in "The Moral Sense" suggested sense of duty as one of the foundations of universal ethics, across all cultures. (Along with sympathy, fairness, and self-control.) It's something most of us feel, more or less, in one way or another. It can be an obligation to a group, which could be a military unit, a street gang, a labor union, an environmental group... It can be an obligation to a social role that we're in, whether we've selected that role or not. Or an obligation to a belief system, like a religion or ideology. A violation of this, e.g., when a soldier runs away, a politician steals money, a criminal snitches on his buddies, a spiritual leader demonstrates less than spiritual behavior, is considered unethical. Because our sense of ethics influences our political orientation, we should consider how this fits into my theory. But sense of duty is probably not a divider between liberal and conservative.

Individual freedom

This is trumpeted often by conservatives and libertarians as their raison d'etre. They want to return to the good old days of the early USA, before Big Government put restrictions on what people can do. But... back in those days, if you were black, you weren't free. If you were female, you were severely restricted in the activities you could undertake. If you did not own property, you could not vote. If you were not Protestant, you could be prevented from holding public office in some states.

But for white male landowners, there was freedom. And possibly this is what conservatives are pining for. The problem with giving freedom to one group, e.g., allowing business owners to decide how safe they want to make their workplaces, means reducing the freedom of another group. So individual freedom questions come down to: whose freedom, and what kind of freedom. E.g., the freedom to own and shoot an automatic pistol vs the freedom of being able to send your kids out to play without worrying they'll be hit by stray bullets. Or the freedom to smoke in a public place, vs the freedom not to have to inhale someone else's smoke.

Like my discussion of individual responsibility above, individual freedom is little more than a political slogan used as a weapon. "We" want freedom, "They" don't. Looking under the surface, it still comes down to EFG.

Why We Believe

Cultural Socialization via Neuro-Plasticity

If you're with me so far, you've discovered -- as I did, after many years of observing politics -- that we all bring our cultural biases to any political issue. Frame of reference, mindset, paradigm, perspective... different terms but the same concept. Our brain is not the tool of rationality that Enlightenment thinkers thought it was.

Some people do realize this. A popular conservative talk-show host claims he makes all his decisions based on instinct. His listeners call themselves "Ditto-heads", presumably because they realize that rational thinking just gets in the way. (A more considered outlook would be one that appreciates how rationality and emotion are mixed, and that one tempers the other.)

There are just countless examples of less-than-rational behavior, in both research settings and real-life. Those who work in the criminal justice system, for instance, know that eyewitness testimony is terribly unreliable, even though it's fodder for TV shows. This is backed up by research. In one famous experiment, a psychology professor had an accomplice burst into his classroom, demand money, and run out. The class was then asked to describe what happened. Fully half the class said the thief was black, even though he had been white. They saw what they expected to see.

In another famous experiment, subjects were asked to watch a video of a basketball practice and count the number of times a basketball was passed among team members. The subjects completely missed that a man in an ape suit wandered through the practice. They just didn't see him because their attention was focused on the ball.

Unrealistic perspectives are a primary cause of political and economic meltdowns. Economists even create differential equations to justify wishful thinking. Then when their mathematical models fail "suddenly", the result is called a "black swan" event or statistical outlier -- something that could not have been predicted. Yet, of course it could -- and was, by people who never bought the distorted perspective in the first place. Conversely, the stock market has its share of "perma-bears" who expect meltdowns constantly, because the beliefs they've adopted tells them it must.

So we're not very rational. But can we be rational when we want to be? Early economists said that when we engage in business transactions, we're rational. But is that even possible? Well, no. Studies in cognitive neuroscience show that when we make a decision, pretty much any decision, both the rational and emotional circuits in our brain are activated. This happens at an unconscious level. Mankind has some degree of free choice and free will, but it's within constraints. And those constraints include brain structure and brain chemistry. "Men make their own history, but they do not make it just as they please, they do not make it under circumstances chosen by themselves, but under circumstances directly encountered, given, and transmitted from the past". (Karl Marx)

So, given that we're not the people we think we should be, according to economists and religious leaders, who are we exactly? The answer is that we're the product of "socialization". This term is a bit vague, but I use it here to mean all the influences on us from birth -- maybe before -- on to the end of life. Those influences are what I labeled culture early on in this book.

The primary mechanism for socialization is what brain researchers like Brian Wexler call "neural plasticity". (Or neuro-plasticity.) The brain actually changes over time. Neural pathways grow or decrease according to external stimuli. That is, everything that happens to us, changes us. Much of this change happens when we're very young, and it comes from our mother or other primary caregiver. Who, consciously and unconsciously, is passing along the culture that she's part of. The brain is most plastic at this age, decreasing over time.

After the mother provides the basic socialization, the process continues with other family members, childhood peers, institutions like schools and churches, pop culture like TV, the work environment -- even individual corporations have a culture -- the military, the local bar.... Hundreds of years ago, a Jesuit priest is reported to have said that if you gave him your child from age 3 to age 8, the child will be his forever. That priest understood the process even if he was unaware of the mechanism. Looked at another way, it's this plasticity that makes mankind adopt to different environments, and evolve.

As we get older, with that plasticity decreasing, instead of our brains changing to match our environment, researchers say we start interpreting -- and even changing -- our environment to match our brains. That's why two people can look at the same thing and "see" it differently

It's the socialization process that accounts for why geography is so important in culture. (The Internet may be changing that a bit.) It's why we have red states and blue states. Geography affects culture which affects our thinking. Including political thinking.

Before we leave this topic, it's worth noting that immigrants bring part of their culture with them, and try to hang on to it even as they want their children to assimilate. The English did this in reverse. When they colonized a country, they wouldn't "go native", which was actually frowned upon, but instead would create a little corner of England in that country. Neither of these are rational things, in the sense that we can consciously control it. It happens at an unconscious level in our brains.

Accepting my theory of empathy vs self-interest and fairness vs social stability, at least for argument's sake, we can see how this leads to other attitudes, political and cultural.

Faith vs reason

Do conservatives typically take things on faith, as I suggested earlier? Faith in traditional religious values, faith in the free market? It would make sense that they do to a greater degree than liberals because the desire to maintain what you've got takes less thinking -- what conservatives would call less "over-intellectualizing" -- than figuring out how to make the current system better/fairer.

Defenders of the status quo know what they're defending. Critics of the status quo may each have their own ideas about what to replace it with. The one requires faith and narrow-mindedness, the other requires the willingness to experiment and the ability to convince others why they should adopt your experiment.

Both liberals and conservative can be ignorant of the facts, i.e., espouse a position without researching it. But it's conservatives who will react positively to a politician who doesn't have any, but whose heart is in the "right" place.

Ends and Means

Conservatives, including hard-line communists, believe that "the ends justify the means". The Bible may bar killing, but can be interpreted to allow exceptions when the goal is desirable, e.g., St. Augustine's "just war". After the Bolshevik Revolution in Russia, the Communists would defend their murderous policies by saying that "you can't make an omelette without breaking eggs". The "Left Opposition" responded with: I see the broken eggs, but where's the omelette?" (Victor Serge)

An alternative position -- not necessarily the "liberal" one, as liberalism just implies a desire for fairness and empathy and doesn't necessarily result in any one outlook -- would be that you can't split apart ends and means. Too often, as in the Soviet Union, the means become the ends. The end is so far away -- and may be impossible to reach -- that you can live your entire life just dealing with "means". So means must be subject to a moral code and to public policy just as ends are. Actions must be taken in context. If it's an immediate life-and-death situation, as in the movie "Unthinkable" or the TV series "24" – how far do you go to stop a terrorist who has rigged a nuclear bomb to explode -- then "emergency ethics" may be justified. (Subject of an essay I wrote.)

The "ends and means" test is an example of people trying to create hard-and-fast rules for ethics, policy, and human behavior in general. That often fails, because the context of the action – both at the time it's happening and when the consequences fall due -- determines the morality. Given that, analyzing an action in terms of empathy and fairness can produce more useful results.

Before leaving this issue, let's take a policy example from WWII: the incarceration of Japanese-Americans. That was done – by liberals, but probably at conservative urging – out of fear, on an end-justifies-the-means basis. It was Us-vs-Them thinking where the "Us" did not include some of our own citizens. Had the policy been considered on grounds of empathy and fairness, that kind of action – in the absence of any evidence suggesting the situation was an emergency -- could not have been justified, as clear heads decided later.

Gender

Political surveys seem to indicate that men and women have a somewhat different orientation on political issues. Conservatives attribute this to self-interest: women being primarily concerned with family issues and men with workplace issues, and then just voting their interest. But there's more to it than that. Males and females are socialized differently -- they receive different stimuli -- different influences -- starting from when they've very young and continuing throughout their lives. Gender roles form a kind of subculture within a larger culture.

In talking about male-female differences we fall into the controversial area of heredity vs environment. At the current level of science, it's almost impossible to separate the two – and in fact their interaction may make them impossible to separate. Fortunately, for the purposes of this book, it's not necessary. In this book, we're not concerned with why men and women are different, but rather what those differences are. For instance, in sports or any competitive game, researchers say that males will generally resolve a dispute by resorting to the rulebook. Females will often resolve a dispute by seeking a resolution that doesn't hurt anyone's feelings. For females, relationships are often more important than a particular game, while that approach is too touchy-feely for many males.

In EFG terms, females are opting for empathy over fairness, and males the reverse. (While mentioning gender differences, I need to back up and point out that overall cultural differences, such as rural vs suburban, can override gender differences.)

Interestingly, what neither males nor females are doing in my game scenario is opting for what I've been calling the politically conservative solutions of self-interest and stability. That is, any solution to the dispute in which certain players -- perhaps those with more money -- can make their own rules, will not be accepted by the players. (Though those same players will accept it if we call the game "business".) Also, any solution based on that's-the-way-we've-done-it-before will not be accepted if the old way is viewed as "wrong". E.g., if players have always cheated, that doesn't mean that cheating should be grand-fathered into the game and trump the written rules.

This is probably a good place to point out that too much empathy results in altruism, a.k.a. a "bleeding heart", which can be self-destructive if taken to an extreme. E.g., if you're one of two guys courting the same girl, having empathy for your competitor is not productive. An example from politics was the belief of 1970s liberals in the rehabilitative powers of the prison system, resulting in easy parole and short sentences for convicts. (In opposition to a more conservative rationale for a prison system: to keep society safe.) Like everything else in life, balance is needed.

Now consider the hero who sacrifices himself to save others. Even though we could consider that altruism taken to an extreme, we all honor it. And probably we do so because we understand that the individual is defending his group: family, military buddies, co-religionists, etc. Again, we can note the difference between the conservative and the liberal is the size of the group the individual will sacrifice for.

I'd like to warn readers that even though I may sometimes couch some conclusions in absolute terms, the real world is way too messy for absolutes. Human behavior is so diverse that words like "never" or "always" are often misleading. (I like the word "often", even though this loses some points for me among those socialized into a firm belief in writings that lay down absolute rules.) Think of guidelines, not rules. And the number of cases falling outside the guidelines, and even far outside, can be considerable. But not so considerable, hopefully, that the guideline is not useful. (Maybe even better is Prof. Scott E. Page's concept of a "cognitive toolbox".)

Age

If you've been doing something for many years, and especially if you've expressed positive opinions on that something -- whether it is music, art, clothing, hairstyle -- it can be upsetting to see young people doing it differently. You may interpret this, perhaps unconsciously, as their saying that what you've been doing all your life has been wrong. (If it wasn't wrong, how come they're not doing the same?) But, really, young people have to do their "own thing" because that's how they make their mark in the world.) Physicist Max Planck is reported to have said that "A new scientific truth does not triumph by convincing its opponents and making them see the light, but rather because its opponents eventually die, and a new generation grows up that is familiar with it."

Progress comes from confronting existing ways of thinking, rather than going along with them. Yet, because we are not the rational creatures we think we are, the older we get, and the more we've been doing things a certain way, the more we find it difficult to be flexible. We become conservative: valuing stability over fairness. In a political story about the health care issue, an elderly woman objected to government intrusion into health care, because that could upset her Medicare coverage. As a policy in effect for 40+ years, Medicare has become an integral part of our world. The issue here is not, as libertarians would have it, between big government and the free market, it's about resistance to change. That resistance tends to increase the older we get.

Mental Toughness

Among Americans, "staying the course" is associated with being tough, while vacillation is associated with weakness. After all, it does take toughness to persevere over all obstacles -- to continue doing what needs to be done no matter what. And those who aren't sure enough of themselves to set a single course make it impossible for others to follow them, as the prospective followers won't know from day to day what the leader's position is. Conservatives will often consider themselves as John Wayne types mowing down obstacles while castigating liberals as flip-floppers.

What conservatives are missing here is that it's only vacillation when you change your mind in the absence of new information. But when you do get new information, such as the U.N. inspectors not finding any WMDs in Iraq, it's not vacillation to change your mind, but flexibility. Admitting a mistake and changing your direction often takes more toughness then to keep doing what you had been doing. (As I've said elsewhere, everyone makes mistakes, it's what you do when you discover you've made one that's important.) Which is tougher for an alcoholic: to refuse to admit he's an alcoholic and keep on drinking, or to admit it and stop drinking?

Ironically, in some of Wayne's best movies, like "The Searchers" and "The Man Who Shot Liberty Valance", the Wayne character followed a traditional path for most of the movie, but then realized it was wrong and did the right thing in the end. In "Liberty Valance", doing the "right thing" cost him everything, but I suspect the character could not have lived with himself if he'd simply kept on doing what he had been doing.

A simple example of changing your mind when conditions change would be a baseball coach who brings in a relief pitcher when his starter isn't getting the job done. Abraham Lincoln faced a similar situation at the beginning of the Civil War. He took some heat for trying one commanding general after another, but what he was doing was getting rid of those who proved they couldn't do the job, until he found someone who could. And then he stuck with Ulysses S. Grant for the remainder of the war, despite criticism of Grant's personal history.

Stereotypical "toughness" must also be appropriate to the situation. In a TV commercial, insurance company Geico shows what happens when a drill instructor finds work as a psychotherapist. (Not good.) Successful corporate executives generally learn when to be tough and when to back off. The same goes for politics. The political leader who insists on following a winner take all policy instead of looking for win-win solutions will generally fail in the end.

I bring up the "toughness" question -- which often is really a question of rigid thinking vs flexibility -- because it seems to have become so identified with conservative vs liberal issues. From what you've read so far, you can surmise that this division can be traced back to a cultural base. Conservatives come from a culture prizing rigid adherence to traditional values in spite of changing conditions -- "You can't change my mind with facts!" -- while liberals come from a culture that prizes re-evaluation and revision. (You can see echoes of the debate between religion and science here.)

In EFG terms, this inflexibility stems from a desire to maintain social stability. Because that desire is the opposite of fairness, decisions are made that are totally unfair, such as destroying the infrastructure of Iraq, creating a million refugees in the process, largely because of a dislike of one man. This harks back to a biblical concept of justice, such as when God got ticked off at Egypt's pharaoh, and got back at him by killing uncounted numbers of Egyptian children. We have indeed progressed to where we no longer target civilians in bombing as we often did in WWII, but there's still not enough recognition or concern for the long-term effects of such bombing -- too much pseudo-toughness and not enough fairness or empathy.

Dogma and Ideology

I've touched on ideology a couple of times before without really getting into it. Because ideology is very relevant to political orientation, we should look at it in more detail. This is not easy, as there are varying definitions of just what an ideology is. Some use it to mean a way of thinking without which it would be difficult to put anything into perspective. An alternative is to view it as a dogmatic belief system: "a system of ideas which systematically misrepresent reality".

The first definition is vague enough to apply to almost anything, and so really isn't interesting. The second definition is the one that relates to this book, because we can see it play out every day on TV talk shows, political speeches, radio call-ins, and so on.

It's when people hold an unmovable position that makes perfect sense to them but little sense to others operating from a different perspective. And cannot be changed by facts.

Essentially, ideological -- or religious -- beliefs are based on faith. Where does that faith come from? If you've been with me so far, you know my answer is the socialization process into a particular culture or subculture. This why ideology, and religion, often seem based in geography. It's why we have red states and blue states, Christian countries and Moslem countries. And why the minority in a country almost always has to fight for acceptance as equals or even just toleration.

Examining ideology, and religion, is a problem that many sociologists have stumbled over. How can you objectively analyze a group that you're a member of, or a group that your group treats as outsiders?

We can take a stab at this by establishing a standard of analysis, and that standard of analysis in this book is the EFG. Let's start with a statement about an ideology, capitalism, by a conservative theologian, the Rev. Emil Brunner: "Capitalism is irresponsibility developed into a system."

By capitalism, what is meant here is not the total politico-economic system the US has in 2011 – which is a mix of capitalistic elements and social welfare elements. (Virtually every other country in the world has such a mix, but in differing amounts.) But rather the belief that a business firm should be run for the monetary benefit of the investors, without regard to the needs of workers, customers, suppliers or the general public. And one in which government does nothing to help others with a stake in the activities of the business.

I've taken some flack for saying that capitalism, even 19th century capitalism, is without empathy. But you don't have to read Dickens to come to that conclusion. For instance, there was no public sanitation in major cities until disease outbreaks that started among the immigrant slums spread to the wealthy, motivating their self-interest.

Pretty much any "ism" is an ideology of some sort, and capitalism is not only not an exception to that, but you can tell from how angry people get when capitalism is criticized that, for many, it's a belief held, not because the holder has extensively studied socioeconomics and history and determined this is the "best" system now and in the future, but because it's an integral part of his culture.

So, proceeding, then where does capitalism fall on the EFG? The more capitalistic a system is, the more concentration on making a profit, under the misreading of Adam Smith that if business owners make a profit, everyone benefits. As Karl Polanyi showed in "The Great Transformation", a work on British economic history also relevant to American history, the more Britain turned to capitalism, the more the general public objected. In the US, the capitalist dependence on child labor, on working employees till they dropped, on paying as little as possible, on dumping toxic waste wherever it was cheapest... was viewed by society in general in a very negative way. This produces what Polanyi called the "double movement": each "advance" in capitalism produced an opposite reaction by society to tame that advance.

With that in mind, we can see that full-blown capitalism scores effectively zero on empathy, because empathy doesn't contribute to profit. And very low on fairness, because business owners only need to be fair if it gets them some advantage. E.g., offering a fair wage when there are competitors, but cutting the wage when you've put your competitors out of business.

In the U.S., we have what used to be called a mixed economy, until the Soviet Union made socialism a dirty word. We have non-capitalist policies like social security, medicare, unemployment compensation, minimum wage laws, pollution regulations, safety regulations, and so on. That gives the system, overall, a higher EFG value than if it was a true capitalist system. It also produces the endless tug of war between those for whom capitalism is part of their culture and those socialized into a subculture with higher EFG values.

Libertarianism is a related ideology. In libertarian thought, freedom is redefined in the negative, as the absence of government "interference" in the economy, rather than as a positive, e.g., the ability to fulfill your potential as individuals. Throughout history, it's hard to think of a single situation where government and business were not interlocked – because those who have obtained economic power will seek political influence, and those with political power will seek economic benefits. Nonetheless, libertarian theory assumes this division exists and proceeds from there.

So, does ideology trump EFG? Because someone is a libertarian, and makes political decisions based on libertarian philosophy, does that mean that this is a case where ideology really does determine political orientation? I'm an ex-libertarian myself. But I ran into something called cognitive dissonance. It's when something becomes harder and harder to believe because reality gets in the way. The thing that got in the way, for me, was a perspective heavily influenced by a cultural background that prized empathy and fairness. Because libertarianism is a system that rewards "the best", with "best" often being determined by money and opportunity, it easily turns into elitism, at odds with empathy and fairness.

Even if everyone were somehow to start out even – 100% estate taxes for instance -- the alpha male types will come out ahead. Which means that you get a system that essentially benefits about 10% of the population, with the remaining 90% hoping the top 10% doesn't exploit them too badly.

I do have to conclude that the simple answers offered by some ideologies can certainly have at least a short-term effect on political orientation. So this is a seeming exception to the EFG method. Yet, at the same time, you can have people adopting an ideology out of a rejection of the culture they were socialized into. As well as people turning to an ideology because it fits their culture. (Do the children of libertarians grow up to be libertarians?)

In any case, we can still use EFG to understand the core beliefs of an individual or group: what lies beneath the veneer of a purely (non-ethical) politico-economic ideology like libertarianism.

Now, to be fair :-) we should examine socialism. This is often an ideology, as well. Adherents to socialism often brook no criticism of it, the hallmark of an ideology. A classic case of blindness of this sort was by an otherwise well-respected academic who believed that Pol Pot should not be criticized for his Cambodian massacres, because the US government had also committed crimes in Southeast Asia. If you got socialized as a child, as I did, with the belief that "two wrongs" don't make a right", it's hard to make sense of a defense like that. The only way to understand it, is to look at the culture that would spawn it. And by culture, just to reinforce what I've said before, I mean not just what we have in our environs when we're growing up, but the environment we're in when we're older.

If you're an academic surrounded by students who write down whatever you say, it can be hard to step back and be self-aware. It can also be very hard to admit a mistake in what you've been telling students for years. (Among stock market traders, this is called guru-itis, referring to someone who's made a good call on the market, and then surrounded himself with people who agree with everything he says, so that he no longer has anyone to question his decisions.) Academics do get to be nit-picked to death by their peers, so the situation isn't as bleak as I've suggested.

But, back to socialism. Defining socialism is much harder than defining capitalism. Sometimes, socialism is defined as government ownership of the means of production and distribution. (By that definition, then Karl Marx wouldn't be a socialist, as we noted earlier, because he had little use for government.) If that's the definition, then socialism eliminates the main engine of productivity, which is the complex system we call the market. (Often this is preceded by the word "free", but it's better for most of us if it's preceded by the word "fair", instead.)

"Complex system" requires its own definition. Complexity Theory states, more or less, that individual agents can interact with each other to self-organize, producing a system with "emergent" features not present in the individual agents. That is, the whole is different than the sum of its parts – because the parts interact with each other. As an example: Prof. Stephen P. Hinshaw notes that consciousness is one such emergent property, as individual neurons don't think.

If you have some different kinds of ants who each know how to do one thing, what do you have? Not just a bunch of ants, but an anthill. If you have a cattle rancher, a butcher, a farmer, a miller, and a baker, what do you have? Maybe a roast beef sandwich.

The drawback, of course, is that such an unsupervised self-organizing system doesn't necessarily lead to an optimal solution. In fact, I would argue that the free market is only free for business owners, and not employees, producing what I would call "anthill economics" – where workers, who are expendable, toil on behalf of the queen. (Or, in modern terms, the king of the hill.)

Drawbacks aside, complex systems – the wisdom of crowds, so to speak -- seem far more productive than top-down systems like state socialism.

State socialism should be open to as much criticism as anything else, but historically it often hasn't been. From the very start of the Soviet Union, criticism of it by other socialists was muted. This was often done by those who viewed communism as being locked in a death struggle with the West, and so any criticism of communism was viewed as giving ammunition to its enemies. As you might expect, this abandonment of the truth led to a kind of moral bankruptcy on the part of many socialists who found themselves on the side of a government with a propensity to commit mass murder.

Neither Nazi Germany nor the Soviet Union ever hit rock bottom on the EFG. Perhaps because both did understand that while the power elite can amass all of a country's resources to itself, it opens itself to revolution if it actually does. Perhaps a Soviet expert can tell us if Soviet policy in providing a social safety net was based on empathy and fairness, or just expediency. (Perhaps similar to how American corporations donate money to charitable causes in the hope of increasing good will.)

Then there're the other variations of socialism. This can get fairly complicated and beyond the scope of this book. Suffice it to say that every such variant can be judged on its EFG, with the judge's criterion being: how close is it to my own EFG. Yes, it might be nice to judge these things with a computer's rationally, but the human brain is not a rational instrument, so we make judgments as human beings. Actually, I think few of us would really want to have things decided by computer -- unless the computer was programmed to behave empathetically and fairly

-- but wait, we already have such a computer in our heads.

I've largely skipped over religion in this discussion of ideology, mostly because those who are religious think of dogma as a positive. Unlike ideologues who think they are being reasonable, the devout believe that faith trumps reason. On the EFG, that can lead the religious conservative to a different place than the economic conservative. For the former, maintaining the current order of things is paramount, with the amount of empathy varying with the religious belief. For the latter, the economic conservative, self-interest is paramount, with typically little empathy for others. The religious conservative and economic conservative can get in bed together on issues that pit them against liberals, but essentially a union between those who worship God and those who think the $ is God, is just a political compromise.

To sum up, then, how ideology and the EFG interact: ideology is part of our socialization process. We think we arrive at an ideology for rational reasons, but the human brain just isn't that rational. We arrive at the ideology because of culture, and the EFG can be used to determine the political orientation of a particular culture. It can also be used to analyze different ideologies. Because the EFG gets to the heart of who we are as individual human beings, it can tell us what's really going on in many political discussions.

Theories in General

"It is a capital mistake to theorize before one has data. Insensibly, one begins to twist facts to suit theories instead of theories to suit facts". (Arthur Conan Doyle via Sherlock Holmes)

In proving a hypothesis, we run up against the socialization process I mentioned above: seeing what we expect to see. (True as well for theories of socialization itself.) As I've noted earlier, we all operate with a mindset which is both responsible for much of our unconscious thought and which guides our conscious thought.

This mindset makes it hard to prove theories. It's particularly difficult if we start with the theory and then look for data to prove it, because we will be unconsciously looking for specific things, i.e., thinking inside the box, to re-use an overworked -- but important -- concept. Not impossible, though. We can have a group of unrelated people collect and examine the data. (See James Suroweiki's The Wisdom of Crowds.) And/or we can try to be aware of our biases and try to be as balanced as we can.

Most scientists, physical and social, will say that you need a theory to start with, as it gives you a guide to what to look at. But in some fields, notably history and cultural anthropology, the researcher throws himself into the data first, then comes up with a "grounded" theory to explain it. That's what I've tried to do here. Your duty as a critical reader, and all reading should be critical, is to identify where I may have gone wrong.

The Upshot

In the long term is there a winner between conservatives and liberals? In a static, unchanging world, conservatives would win. But population growth, innovation, climate change, and a host of other factors make maintaining total social stability an impossible task. But conservatives can slow down the rate of social change -- the rate at which society responds to these pressures. From a liberal point of view, that's not a good thing. :-) But for the average person, who can only take so much change at a time, it's not bad.

For liberals, winning means accepting that there is always one step backwards for every two steps forward. (Or 2 steps backwards for every 3 steps forwards, according to R.N. Elliott.) But fighting to keep that one step backwards from becoming the status quo, as has been happening since the Reagan era. It's making history into a progression and not a cycle, and certainly not a regression.

We've seen progress happen in the West since the fall of the Roman Empire: with Roman domination removed, national cultures developed, roads could go somewhere else other than to Rome.... :-) Over the last two hundred years, liberals have fought to end slavery, end child labor, provide public education, end racial segregation, and a host of other things that advocates of the status quo have fought against, often bitterly and even violently. But in time these things became part of the status quo and became acceptable to conservatives.

Both liberals and conservatives have the capability of being self-aware, of understanding why they have the political orientation they do, and why the other guy has his. But if you think that this will help reach compromises, that may be hoping too much. After all, those with limited empathy, even if they understand what the other guy wants, are not going to care.

Some professional mediators say that compromises often don't work because neither side really gets what it wants. But that you can get a win-win situation if both parties realize they're part of the same team with the same goals. I think for politics, though, the only time the goals are the same is when responding to an external threat. Other than that, this is an eternal conflict. That's life.

While I've pointed out defects in conservatism in this book, we should realize that conservatism is necessary in certain situations. In a military battlefield situation, you don't want your soldiers to feel any empathy for their enemy. That's fatal, because shooting first is often necessary for self survival. During WWII, the military and the government in general demonized the Japanese in order to avoid any such feelings of empathy. (Easier to do with the Japanese than with the Germans, because of the obvious ethnic difference.)

This works less well with insurgencies where the soldier has entered a country to help the people there and must distinguish between civilian and enemy. The lack of empathy that was valuable in WWII works against him here, increasing civilian abuse and even deaths vs more empathetic soldiers. Essentially, it's the difference between soldiering and policing. Even though the essence of a policing function is to maintain order, a lack of fairness and empathy will increase civilian hostility and make the job harder. Not to mention offending Americans hearing about abuses who are operating with an empathy-fairness mindset.

The criminal justice system by its nature is conservative. It's human to expect that people who deal with criminals every day are going to rank low on any empathy scale. (Even if they started out being empathetic, they could well become resocialized after many years.) So, we don't free a killer because he had a bad childhood. But we may hire a social worker, who scores high on empathy, to try and prevent kids from becoming killers.

The educational system is conservative. We instruct our children into the standards of our society. In history, for instance, we give them a narrative of how we got to where we are: the obstacles overcome, our heroes, our traditions.... Many, if not all textbooks, ignore the controversies in a field in order to present that single narrative. Whereas, in real life, not just in history, but in social science in general, in physical science, and in the humanities, controversy is rampant. And what's in favor at any one time is subject to revision. This revisionism does drive conservatives crazy, because every revision is a change to the current order of things. But without it, we would still be thinking the Sun revolves around the Earth.

In general, institutions resist change, even liberal ones. It's the nature of an institution, especially a bureaucracy, to put the self-interest of the organization above that of the purpose for which the organization was originally created.

Lawrence Harrison, writing in The Central Liberal Truth, thinks that culture can be changed to be more in tune with progress and development. But what you consider progress is going to depend on your cultural background.

So, while culture can change – after all, few believe in slavery any more -- essentially, conservatism will always be with us. And liberalism is with us in the modern world because it's not possible for conservatives to keep the world from changing, as it was in medieval societies. It's also true, as Prof. Page has pointed out in The Difference, that diversity trumps homogeneity. A group of people with diverse perspectives are more likely to arrive at a useful solution to a problem than a group of people who all think the same way. (Though he also points out that differing goals can make it harder to arrive at a solution.)

Perhaps the most important conclusion to be drawn from all this is that we should be aware of motivations: to have the self-awareness to understand why we believe what we do and why we take the actions we do, and to be empathetic enough to understand why others believe and act as they do.

Epilogue

I wrote this book to work out in my own head where political orientation comes from, and then see if I can explain it to others. It's helped me understand political issues better. It's also affected the way I see some popular entertainment. .In watching reruns of the 2003-2005 fantasy TV series "Tru Calling", for instance, where Tru saves people who are supposed to die, while Jack tries to prevent her from doing that because he believes such change is bad for the natural order of things, I can see the same fairness vs social stability issue I've talked about here.

Ditto for the imaginative 1997-2001 TV series La Femme Nikita, where Nikita's empathy is a liability to herself, as she's forced to work for a counter-terrorist organization that has none. Or maybe, my new paradigm is making me interpret things the writers didn't intend. :-)

In my own local area, there is a controversy over whether the Washington Redskins football team should keep their name or not. Even though this is not a political issue, opinion pretty cleanly divides into liberal and conservative: with liberals taking the side of those who are offended by the name and conservatives trying to keep things as they always have been. We can clearly see here the desire to maintain a tradition no matter how unfair it is. Liberals offer the fairness argument that if it was some other ethnic group that was being denigrated, we wouldn't allow it – an argument that is meaningless to those who don't prize fairness very highly.

I should note, in passing, that I'm not an academic, as if you couldn't tell. :-) I just read a lot. This can be an advantage, as I can integrate research across multiple fields without being expected to concentrate on a particular specialty.

I do though, have an orientation towards something I call cognitive history. Which is the study of why people in the past did what they did, what was going on in their heads when they did it, and why did they think/believe what they did. This is not a real academic specialty, undoubtedly because it's way too speculative for mainstream historians. And it is in fact highly speculative. But it can produce some great insights into human behavior that are relevant today.

This book is a work in progress -- and I'm interested in reader input. You can email with comments, critiques, suggestions, etc., to ericbalkan@yahoo.com. Put something interesting in the subject line so I'll notice it in my inbox. Avoid using words like free, mortgage, or enlargement.

Addendum A: Reading List

Some interesting further reading:

Wexler, Bruce -- Brain and Culture
Iacoboni, Marco - Mirroring People
Zerubavel, Eviatar - Social Mindscapes
Wilson, James Q -- The Moral Sense
Baron-Cohen, Simon -- The Science of Evil: On
    Empathy and the Origins of Cruelty
Surowiecki, James - The Wisdom of Crowds
Polanyi, Karl - The Great Transformation
Fischer, Edward - The Teaching Company: Peoples
    and Cultures of the World
Page, Scott E - The Teaching Company:
    Understanding Complexity. Also The
    Difference
Hinshaw, Stephen P – The Teaching Company:
    Origins of the Human Mind
Grim, Patrick – The Teaching Company: The
    Philosophy of Mind
Bernstein, Jared - All Together Now
Kuhn, Thomas S - The Structure of Scientific
    Revolutions

Addendum B: Analyzing Some Current Issues

We now have tools we can use to analyze political positions. Let's try some hot topics: (Please forgive any rants – that comes with the territory.)

One more thing first: pragmatism. Ideally, the translation of political opinion into political policy should involve considerations of what is practical – what we can actually do. The greatest idea won't work if it can't actually be implemented, That is, if we don't have the time, the money, the people, the knowledge, the will, etc., we probably shouldn't do it, no matter how well-intentioned. "The road to Hell...."

It's also worth bearing in mind – and this is just a personal observation – that most every significant problem has both a short-term and a long-term solution. E.g., the solution for crime short-term is to lock people up. The solution for crime long-term is to give people alternatives to becoming criminals.

OK, then here goes.

1 – Universal health care

Self-interest: "I don't want to be shelling out money for other people, who probably don't deserve it." (Note some residual fairness here.)

Social stability: "If we monkey with the system, we'll ruin it for everyone."

Fairness: "Why should health care be based on how much money we make? Imagine running police and fire departments that way, or public education."

Empathy: "Why punish children because their parents don't have insurance? And those people could be us, in different circumstances."

Tempering this with pragmatism could mean being reasonably sure that the changes we implement won't make things worse.

2 – Health care costs

In "Overtreated", science writer Shannon Brownlee provides page after page of descriptions of how Americans pay more for less, than people in any other developed country. How do we fix this? Do we want to fix this?

Doctors (especially specialists), hospitals, and insurance companies argue against change, based on self-interest and resistance to change. The other side, essentially those who favor single-payer systems, have not gotten much attention. But you can figure that argument is based on typical liberal grounds of fairness and empathy. Perhaps they should appeal to conservatives by adding self-interest into the mix.

3 – Gay marriage

Liberals have approached this issue by appealing to people who have supported them in the past. But, as they say, "politics make strange bedfellows". For example, minority group leaders that lobby for more government economic assistance may be doing it out of self-interest – a conservative attribute -- rather than liberal grounds of fairness or empathy. So when liberals approach them on the gay marriage issue, especially for those who are deeply religious, liberals will be rebuffed due to the conservative attribute of social stability.

(I offer these opinions as my personal analysis. Your own analysis may lead to different conclusions. Don't take anything I say on faith.)

4 – Wikileaks

This may be a dead issue by the time you read this, but the central point – what should be secret and what shouldn't – is timeless.

You can guess the conservative opinion: Don't rock the boat, and How does this affect me? (With thanks to Al Franken.)

The liberal position -- which should recognize that secrets cause wars, financial meltdowns, worsens natural catastrophes – should be based on empathy and fairness. (And not fall into the conservative trap that if a whistle-blower should go too far, that invalidates everything he's done.)

After Katrina, it was discovered that the Army Corps of Engineers, tasked with building levees for New Orleans, had contracted out the building to private companies. One such company told the Army that they'd picked a bad place to build a levee, because the ground was porous – it would wash away in a storm flood. The Army told the company, according to the news reports I've seen, to just build the levee there anyway. And keep quiet about it.

Too bad this came out after Katrina and not before. If the government is not accountable to the public, who are they accountable to?

Ditto for the manufactured "evidence" gathered by the Bush Administration about WMDs in Iraq or Saddam's bogus ties to Al Qaeda.

Also true for investment banks in an unregulated environment, for legal settlements involving public corporations in which the case is closed to the public, and in general for all those things that can affect us. Apparently, we think it more important to reveal secrets about celebrities' lives than to reveal secrets that can ruin people's lives.

5 - Military intervention overseas

Self-interest: "Do they have oil?"

Social stability: "Does it affect our national security?" E.g., "are they an ally of ours against world terrorism?"

Fairness: "Which side offers liberal democracy?" Despite the fact that two liberal presidents intervened in Vietnam in the 1960s, if this question had been asked, the answer would have been: neither.

Empathy: "Can we prevent suffering?" As I write this, President Obama has just intervened in Libya, stating this reason.

Of course, pragmatism is important. If we can't afford our current overseas military commitments – and it seems we can't – we can hardly take on new ones, at least new long-term ones. To think otherwise, to be idealistic and non-pragmatic, is to be making decisions based on wishful thinking. (Yes, that's a personal opinion.)

6 – The War on Drugs

Self-interest: "Drug addicts commit crimes. Keep drugs out of the US, and punish the addicts."
Social stability: "Drug addiction destroys families. Keep drugs out of the US and punish the addicts."
Fairness: "Drug addiction should be a health issue, not a crime. Even doctors can get hooked on drugs, but they don't end up in prison."
Empathy: "An arrest for drug possession damages a person's chance to get a good job, so even if the addict has recovered, he's classified the same as if he hadn't."

Of course, on pragmatic grounds, the War on Drugs has been a total failure. Not only hasn't it kept drugs out of the country, but it's given us the highest percentage of our population in prison than any other developed country. It's also produced a generation of inner city youths with arrest records, an epidemic of violence in Mexico that could come here, and street violence that's already here...

7 – Jobs

The recovery from the 2001 recession saw some job growth, though not enough to keep the economy growing. (Just to keep up with the growth in the labor force, the US needs to create about 120,000 jobs a month.)

Worse, an analysis of the Bureau of Labor Statistics numbers I did back in 2005 indicated that such growth as there was, was primarily in construction, a cyclical industry, and in mortgage financing – a warning sign I missed. A distant third was retail. Health care was a distant fourth. In this "boom" period, jobs for college graduates showed no growth at all.

In the current "recovery", the stock market is doing great, but there's no apparent job growth in the kind of jobs that America's future depends on. That's not retailing. Or health insurance claims processing.

Self-interest: "If I can get a job, so should everyone else." This changes during an actual recession to: "I'd have a job, if it wasn't for those dang liberals who have ruined the business environment."

Social stability: "Things will work out in the end, if the government doesn't interfere, because everything has always worked out before."

Fairness: "Anyone can be laid off, through no fault of their own. We should be using government to make sure there are jobs for the future, for everyone who wants one."

Empathy: "Too many people are failing through holes in the social safety net, from middle class into poverty. And it's getting harder for those in poverty to find a way out."

Unfortunately, the people we trust to give us good economic advice have let us down. They are mired in 19th century theories of how economics should work, instead of how it actually does work. Protectionism does actually work, and save jobs, while free trade doesn't, and costs jobs. (See Ian Fletcher, "Free Trade Doesn't Work". Also H-J Chang, "Bad Samaritans")

Nor can we trust business leaders to point the economy in the right direction. An estimated 47% of the revenue of the S&P 500 – the 500 largest US public companies – comes from outside the U.S. If a business can make more profit shifting jobs overseas, they will. This helps stock market investors, not US workers.

Liberals need to change the argument to: how do we turn the US economy into a fair economy that benefits everyone, not just investors.

8 – Attacks on Unions

If I can generalize – well, I've been doing that all along, so why stop now, lol – those who place self-interest above everything else are either rich or think they can become rich by dint of their individual initiative. Unions are viewed as an obstacle – they work via collective rather than individual action, they eat into corporate profits (or government revenue) , they interfere with management fire-at-will policies, they're greedy, etc. So, these economic conservatives yearn for a world with no unions.

Feelings about unions:

Self-interest: Bust 'em. Fire 'em all when they strike.

Social stability: Hammer 'em down when they ask for too much

Fairness: necessary, because the individual cannot otherwise deal with a large organization on a level playing field

Empathy: without unions, which invented the concept of weekends off, a living wage, safe working conditions, etc., the quality of life would be a lot lower for many of us.

9 – Public Broadcasting

Self-interest: If they don't reflect my personal views, then I don't need them

Social stability: Non-commercial activities are un-American and strike at the heart of the free enterprise system

Fairness: If you have a message that's worth getting out on the airwaves, but it won't make anyone any money, then public broadcasting is the only option.

> Empathy: This is a necessary option for those who have trouble finding a trusted voice who is not trying to sell them something.

10 – Science vs Religion/Ideology

Self-interest: Science is useful in so far as it results in actual products that I can use, and definitely not in reports of impending doom that will cost me money.

Social stability: Science is OK as long as it doesn't interfere with well-established beliefs in traditional values.

Fairness: If science is subordinated to particular religious or politico-economic values, then people may be deprived of science's benefits who may not even subscribe to those values.

Empathy: Alleviating suffering should take precedence over disputes of one set of values vs another.

Well, that's probably enough. You get the idea. Email me with any you find are hard to analyze.

With the analysis done, where do we go now? What do we do with it?

Having gotten an insight into what determines the liberal and conservative stance on individual issues, we have an idea of how to get people on our side in an issue. If we can identify what of the four goals most drive a person or a group, we can target that motivator.

Let's take health care reform. Studies indicate that Americans pay more money for less care than in any other developed country. The key to get liberal support for change has been to talk about reducing the cost for those not insured, such as by increasing insurance coverage or going to a single-payer system. But that tack has zero interest for conservatives. To get broad-based support for change, a new plan would have to save people money, to appeal to economic self-interest conservatives. And would have to allow anti-change social conservatives the same freedom to pick their own doctors as they have now. It's probably not easy to craft a plan that appeals to all groups, but if it were easy it would have already been done. Note that saving insurance industry profits does not need to be part of the plan in order to get support from conservatives.

Note that this approach is not a compromise, which by nature are nobody-really-wins solutions. This approach looks for a win-win solution. Of course, that's not how politics is done today. Today, the side with the votes attempts to run over the other side to get their legislation enacted, or legislation they don't like repealed. Then when the other side gets more votes, the reverse happens – producing government policy that seems to stumble and lurch in one direction after another.

If this all sounds like liberals should not treat conservatives as the enemy, that's correct. This is not a war, it's a culture clash. Though it's a clash with a culture that does seem to regard liberals as the enemy. And it's often not easy to work with people who may lack the empathy to see the other person's point of view or enough sense of fairness to even give the other person a fair hearing. But that just means that liberals, who **can** accept pluralism in viewpoints, have to work harder to bring people together.

Addendum C: Q & A

Additional thoughts keep coming to me, but as this work grew it became harder to fit them into what I had already written and still have the narrative flow smoothly. (Or as smoothly as I could make it.) So I've decided to add a Q&A section where I add more points and also address any potential concerns. (Email me with any questions – my email address should be at the end of the book. If they're of general concern, I'll add them to this section.)

Q. When someone does things for others that makes himself feel good, isn't he then acting out of self-interest – just out of the pleasure-pain principle?

A. In a sense, yes, but that's not a particularly useful definition of self-interest. If we refer to people helping others as self-interest, what term do we use to refer to people who pursue their own desires regardless of the effect on others? CEOs? :-) The difference between these two two types of motivations is the degree of empathy. My thesis argues that in looking at a political issue, we can attempt to ascertain which side of the issue is most in accord with our own degree of empathy. And why others with a different degree of empathy may take a different position.

Q. Aren't we all capable at one time or another of some act that shows a lack of empathy?

A. From time to time, we can be caught in the grasp of some powerful emotion: greed, fear, lust, self-preservation, anger, etc. – which seems to override our usual behavior, e.g., our empathy. The result is that we say or do something that's hurtful to another, which we regret later. And that's the key: that we regret it later. If we really had little or no sense of empathy – because we had rationalized it away or overridden it with dogma or we didn't have any in the first place -- we wouldn't regret it.

Q. Is it a new idea that people hold their beliefs for unconscious reasons?

A. The idea has gotten more attention "recently" with developments in cognitive neuroscience, but the concept has been discussed in philosophy and social science for a long time. American philosopher, William James, began his classic work Pragmatism (1907) by noting this.

"For the philosophy which is so important in each of us is not a technical matter; it is our more or less dumb sense of what life honestly and deeply means." And this leads a man (or woman) to "... see things, see them straight in his own peculiar way, and be dissatisfied with any opposite way of seeing them. There is no reason to suppose that this strong temperamental vision is from now onward to count no longer in the history of man's beliefs". And:

"Of whatever temperament a professional philosopher is, he tries when philosophizing to sink the fact of his temperament. Temperament is no conventionally recognized reason, so he urges impersonal reasons only for his conclusions. Yet his temperament really gives him a stronger bias than any of his more strictly objective premises. It loads the evidence for him one way or the other, making for a more sentimental or a more hard-hearted view of the universe, just as this fact or that principle would. He trusts his temperament. Wanting a universe that suits it, he believes in any representation of the universe that does suit it. He feels men of opposite temper to be out of key with the world's character, and in his heart considers them incompetent and 'not in it' in the philosophic business, even tho they may far excel him in dialectical ability."

James extends this analysis to other men of ideas, not just philosophers. Those of us who think about ideas all fall victim to the unconscious workings of the mind. Even those who don't think about ideas have inculcated them from those who do. J.M. Keynes once remarked: "Practical men, who believe themselves to be quite exempt from any intellectual influence, are usually the slaves of some defunct economist." (Or priest.)

I've read of an interesting non-political research finding of this sort. Teachers were told that the students in their class had been given a test which scored them as either high aptitude or low aptitude. And they were given the names of the students in each group. At the end of the term, the children with the highest marks were the ones in the high-aptitude group. That would make sense, except there was no test -- the children had been assigned randomly to the two groups. The teachers had been led to believe something that wasn't true, and this had affected their behavior towards each child. (I think this must have happened some time back, because it seems that modern ethical considerations would prohibit this kind of test.)

Q. Can people change?

A. William James, again, noted that new ideas don't replace old ones, but are integrated into our current beliefs in such a way to keep most of the old ones intact. (Cf the Planck quote earlier.)

Yet, we do have enough free will to effect a change. We may even have a kind of epiphany when something becomes clear for the first time.

Q. Is religious fundamentalism necessarily politically conservative?

A. Strictly speaking, no. If the fundamentals of the religion incorporate empathy and fairness, like the "Social Gospel" of 1900 or "liberation theology" more recently, the result can be politically liberal. But the nature of fundamentalism involves an adherence to the original teachings of a faith. And most modern faiths are fairly old, having developed when concepts of empathy and fairness were different. E.g., when slavery was acceptable, and "convert or die" was much more typical than "live and let live". And so fundamentalism is largely tied to a way of thinking out of place in the modern world of political/religious/ethnic diversity.

A modern example of a fundamentalist who combined competing thoughts was Mother Theresa. (Or, as Christopher Hitchens put it, the "Albanian dwarf") At the same time that Mother Theresa consoled women in poverty, she lashed out at those women who practiced birth control -- ensuring permanent poverty for those she was assumed to be helping. The population of India has doubled every 40 years – it doubled from 1930 to 1970 and again from 1970 to 2011 -- and is long past the Malthusian point where the land can support the population. But Mother Theresa's religion blinded her – as religion and ideology often do – to where considerations of empathy and fairness should have led her.

Q. Empathy leads us to respect diversity. But should we really give political rights and self-determination to, say, a group that advocates our destruction and is just waiting for the means to do so?

A. Empathy can't be absolute. There's a reason we have evolved to also desire social stability. Any society that doesn't will fail. So a balance has to be created. Determining that balance can be tricky – who said life is easy? There are no absolute rules involved. We have to figure out how to protect

ourselves and our institutions while still being fair
and not ignoring our natural empathy.

Q. How does EFG apply to corporations?

A. Corporations operate on the typical
conservative principles of self-interest and social
stability – which often conflict. While neoclassic
economic theory says that the business firm always
seeks a profit, that's not really what goes on.

As a number of recent business failures attest,
e.g., the investment banking firms, the self-interest
involved is the self-interest of the CEO and select
employees, and not the company as a whole. Or,
often, it's the self-interest of the investors rather than
the good of the firm. Some modern companies like
Amazon and Goggle have been hammered by
investors because they set their goal to be long-term
success, while investors have become used to the
normal method of doing business in America – which
is to concentrate on the next quarter's profit figures so
as to create a short-term bump in the stock price.

The other corporate goal is something pointed
out years ago by C. Northcote Parkinson (Parkinson's
Law, 1957) – that the primary goal of any
bureaucracy is to maintain its own existence. (Any
large organization, including large corporations, is
bureaucratic.) That's why, when banks, handed
billions of dollars by the Treasury and the Fed to
continue making loans during the recent financial

crisis, instead used the money to pay down debt, to make themselves more secure. That was a good survival instinct, but the failure of our government leaders to take this into account led to misdirected policies.

The upshot here is that corporations, not being human, do not get upset by unfairness and do not feel empathy for others. Some of their management and investors may, but the system is structured to make those feelings irrelevant. Those who rise to the top of a corporate bureaucracy are those with an eye on self-interest, not fairness. A recent movie, "Made in Dagenham", shows British women on strike in 1968 for equal pay with the men – and having enormous trouble in getting management to realize the unfairness of the existing system.

Q. Conservatism has been described as taking the "traditions and values of the past and applying them to the future". (Patrick N. Allitt) Do you agree with that?

A. I think that's a fairly apt description, as far as it goes. Where that differs from liberalism is that liberals want to take the values of the present and apply them to the future. (Or at least the liberal values of fairness and empathy.) Take two government programs that have been part of modern society for several decades now, social security and Medicare. Liberals see those programs as providing a current value, and so concentrate on how they could be improved for the future. Whereas staunch conservatives, particularly those who look back fondly on the days of the Founding Fathers or the "rugged individualism" of 19th century pioneers, see a society where those programs didn't exist – and so are unconvinced of their value, no matter what facts are presented.

Those conservatives stuck in the past often have an idealized vision of that past. The values and traditions of the past included slavery, child labor, racial segregation, environmental degradation, religious discrimination, gender discrimination.... Sure, some values of the past were worthwhile, but those are the ones we kept. The ones we didn't keep, we generally didn't keep for a reason.

This is not to say that we have always gone in the right direction, but the way to find the right direction is to figure it out using our sense of empathy and fairness – rather than turn to values and traditions that may no longer work.

Q. You seem to imply that libertarianism is closely related to conservatism. Don't they differ on key principles?

A. At one time, like back in the 1960s, libertarians could be (logically) divided themselves into Left-Libertarians and Right-Libertarians. As time went on, though, and with corporate money flowing towards Right-Libertarians, culminating in the creation of the Cato Institute and the takeover of the Libertarian Party by "the suits", Right-

Libertarianism became the only kind that today gets any attention.

Here's a libertarian "litmus-test". Given that The State (government) should not interfere in the economy, according to libertarians, and corporations are creations of the State and are given special rights by The State (in both federal and state courts), should a Libertarian president dissolve corporations? If the libertarian answers no, then clearly he has placed social stability above any other consideration – and that makes him a lot more like conservatives than he may think he is.

Q. How do we decide what's fair? Don't we all have different opinions on that?

A. We seem to all have a built-in mechanism for determing what's unfair. Experiments with other primates have shown that it's upsetting, for instance, to get a lesser reward for a task than another individual who did the same task.

The essence of a jury trial, to give another example, is that observers, chosen to be unbiased, will come to a fair decision once given the facts. That's essentially a good idea, though sometimes the execution of the idea needs improvement.

Philosopher John Rawls, in The Theory of Justice, asked us to imagine someone behind a "veil of ignorance", as a way of ensuring impartiality. (Though his intended use for the concept is different than mine.) That is, if we are unaware of our personal interests and so don't know which side in a dispute would benefit us, we won't be favoring one side or the other. Well, that's a thought-experiment that could be hard to implement. But a parent of small children may have actually used that principle. E.g., when dividing a treat between two children, have one child divide the treat while the other child has the first choice over which half to take. That ensures that the first child makes the fairest division possible. I don't know how well that will work in settling the Israeli-Palestinian problem, but it may give us a direction.

Q. Do you ascribe moral values to liberalism vs conservatism, or empathy vs self-interest, or fairness vs social-stability?

A. It's tempting to do that, but it gets complicated. It gets into free-will vs determinism questions, for instance. Because our political orientation is largely the result of our cultural socialization, plus individual genetics and upbringing, and takes quite a determined effort to override it, ascribing a moral judgement to political opinions could be blaming people for attitudes they may not have much control over. It's a topic for another book.

Addendum D: A Mock Discussion

To be fair, I should give "the other side" a chance to respond. (Well, not really.) So, I've invited novelist-philosopher Ima Remington and noted economist Prof Murray von Friedmann of the Dogo Institute, advocates of dog-eat-dog capitalism.

Miss Remington: In my novels and rants, my heroes are elitists. They're smarter and more admirable than, ugh, workers and other ordinary people. Isn't it rational for them to structure the world to serve their own self-interest?

Prof von Friedmann: Right, Miss Remington. It's incorrect to assume that a system which rewards the top 5% is bad. If you're in that top 5% it's good. From the top of the hill, all those people are just ants, so who cares?

EB: Well that's been the case through much of history, but you can understand that those who are left out – who are still living paycheck to paycheck or who face a retirement shortfall – are not going to buy into a system that rewards just the top 5%. Historically, it's meant revolutions, riots, and other civil unrest. Instead, we should be thinking of a system that benefits as many people as it can – both for reasons of fairness and empathy, and for reasons of pragmatism – because that'll work better.

Miss Remington: There are only problems like that because there are people out there who hold opinions different than mine. In my novel, "Atlas Drugged", I depict a world in which the Leader converts the important people of the world over to his way of thinking, which of course is my way of thinking. This is self-interest that is rational, and what makes it rational is that I say it is. Clearly, if someone's thinking differs from mine, it must not be rational, because, when I promote self-interest, I mean, of course, my own self-interest.

EB: The rationality of drinking the Kool-Aid, hmmm.

Prof von Friedmann: In the marketplace of ideas, where voting is by dollars – one dollar, one vote – the ideas of those with the most money to spend win out. And why not? If you have more money, that means you're a more successful person than someone with less money. So why shouldn't you make the decisions for everyone else? Remember, the bedrock of America is being free to choose, from among the choices we give you.

EB: You two are impossibly selfish.

Miss Remington: Thank you for the compliment!

###

Also by Eric Balkan:

Essays on ibrakefortrees.wordpress.com:
    Fair Markets vs Anthill Economics
    The Free Trade Debate

Historical Fiction:
    City of Tears
    Locksley's Crusade

Science Fiction/Fantasy:
    The Good Soldier
    The Third Wish
    Just Cloning Around

To contact the author,
mailto:ericbalkan@yahoo.com

Thanks for reading!

www.ingramcontent.com/pod-product-compliance
Lightning Source LLC
Chambersburg PA
CBHW050547280326
41933CB00011B/1747